How do TOYS Work?

by Joanna Brundle

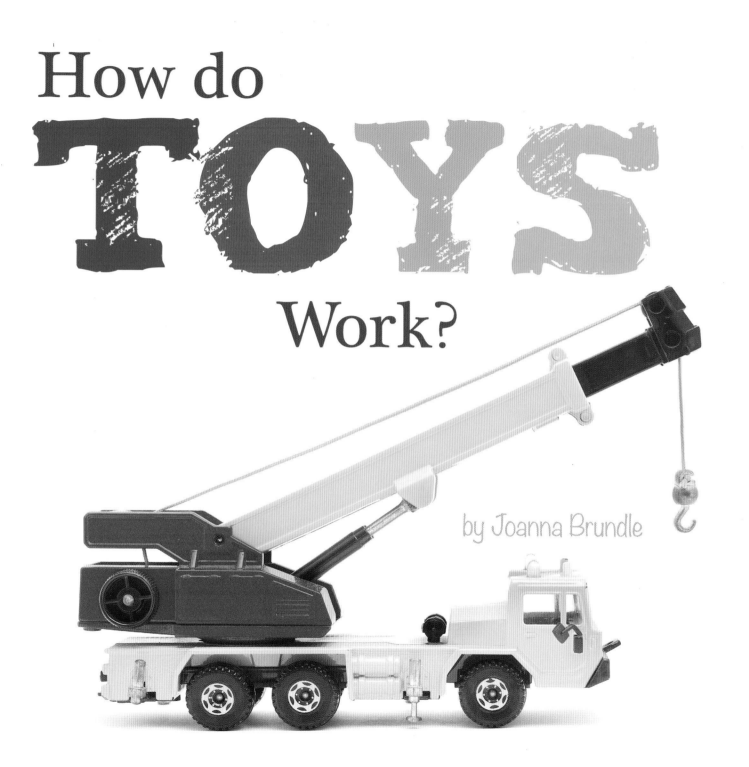

©2016
Book Life
King's Lynn
Norfolk PE30 4LS

ISBN: 978-1-910512-90-6

Written by:
Joanna Brundle

Designed by:
Ian McMullen

A catalogue record for this book
is available from the British Library.

CONTENTS

PAGE	Title
4-5	Clockwork and Wind-up Toys
6-7	Pulleys
8-9	Levers
10-11	Radio-controlled Toys
12-13	Wheels and Axles
14-15	Gears
16-17	Ramps
18-19	Batteries
20-21	Robots and Talking Dolls
22	Fun Things to Do
23	Photo Quiz
24	Glossary and Index

You can find the orange words in this book in the Glossary on page 24.

Clockwork and Wind-up

TOYS

Clockwork and wind-up toys have a spring. Pulling a spring stretches it. Pushing a spring squashes it.

A spring being pulled.

Winding the key squashes the spring inside the robot.

Sitting on the toy squashes the spring.

When you stop pulling or pushing, the spring goes back to its normal shape. This makes the toy move.

Some toys use a pulley. A pulley is a wheel
with a rope or chain wrapped round it.
A pulley is used to lift or lower things.

The pulley lowers the
hook on this toy crane.

6

Sitting on the toy squashes the spring.

When you stop pulling or pushing, the spring goes back to its normal shape. This makes the toy move.

PULLEYS

Some toys use a pulley. A pulley is a wheel with a rope or chain wrapped round it. A pulley is used to lift or lower things.

The pulley lowers the hook on this toy crane.

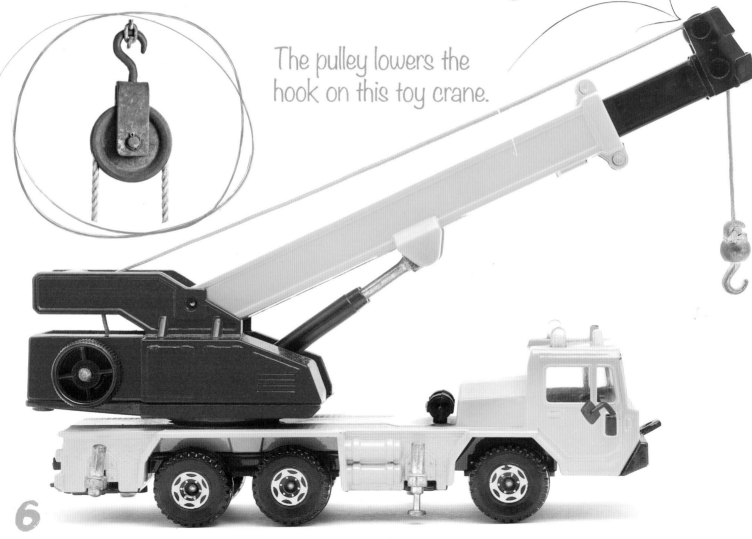

6

Pulleys help us to lift and move heavy things, like bricks on a building site or goods in and out of cargo ships.

Pulley

Hook

A crane uses a pulley to lift and lower the hook.

7

A lever is a tool used to make something move. If you push or pull a lever at one end, it makes the other end move.

The pivot point is the place where something turns. Can you spot the pivot point on this seesaw?

The see-saw is a lever that moves the children up and down.

9

Radio-controlled TOYS

Radio-controlled toys pick up special radio waves that make a motor inside the toy work. The gadget that sends out the special waves is called a transmitter.

Your radio at home also picks up waves that make sounds.

Helicopter

Car

Transmitter

Examples of radio-controlled toys include model cars, aeroplanes and helicopters. They all need power. Power comes from a battery pack.

Wheels and AXLES

Can you imagine trying to push or pull a dolls pram or ride-on tractor if it had no wheels, or wheels that were square? Wheels make this toy move easily and smoothly because they are round and turn freely.

Wheels make this toy easy to push.

12

An axle is a rod or bar which connects the wheels. If the axle is fixed, the wheels spin. If the wheels are fixed, the axle spins. Together, they make the toy move.

Wheel

Axle

The axle on this skateboard is fixed. The wheels spin freely.

GEARS

Gears are wheels with teeth around the edges. Gears can fit together and the teeth stop them slipping. When one gear turns, the others turn too. Gears take power from one part of a toy to another.

Can you see how turning one gear will make another part of this toy move?

Teeth

Gears of different sizes can be joined together to increase speed. Turning a big gear slowly turns a joined small gear more quickly. This is what happens when you change gear on your bicycle.

Gears take power from the pedals to the back wheel.

Pedal

RAMPS

A ramp is a flat surface, raised up at an angle. A marble run is a good example. At the top of the ramp, the marble has stored energy, which is released as moving energy when you let go.

A marble run

Ramp

A garden slide is a ramp.

The force of **gravity** pulls the marble, or you, down the ramp. Look at the ramps in this toy garage. The cars speed up, the further down the ramp they go. This is called acceleration.

Ramp

BATTERIES

Many toys use batteries to work. A battery is a container for storing energy or power. When the battery is used, this stored power changes to electrical energy. Toy animals that move, model racing cars and children's tablets are all powered by batteries.

Tablets usually have a special power pack called a lithium battery

This toy car has a rechargeable battery pack in the boot.

Some batteries run out of power and have to be replaced. Other batteries can be plugged into **mains electricity** to top up their supply of power. They are called rechargeable batteries.

ROBOTS
and Talking
DOLLS

Robots are **man-made** but they copy how we and animals behave. Many robots are powered by batteries and have a computer brain.

Early talking dolls had a string at the back. Pulling the string squashed a spring inside the doll. The spring then turned a disc to play sounds through a speaker. Modern talking dolls produce electronic sounds.

Modern baby dolls gurgle and cry like real babies.

21

FUN
Things
TO DO

Get on a see-saw with a friend. Be careful and hold on tightly! What happens if you both sit very close to the middle? What happens if one of you moves to the end?

Try letting your toy cars go down a ramp. What happens if you let go of them higher up the ramp? Put the ramp on carpet, then on a smooth floor. What happens when the cars come off the ramp?

Take a look at your toys at home or in your classroom. Do any of them use a spring?

PHOTO QUIZ

Look at these photos. One of these toys uses a spring, one uses a lever and one uses wheels and an axle. Which is which? (Answer on page 24)

A

B

C

GLOSSARY

MAN-MADE
Not natural, made by humans

GRAVITY
A force which pulls everything downwards towards the centre of the Earth

MAINS ELECTRICITY
Power supplied to our homes by wires or cables

ANSWERS

A Wheel and axle

B Spring

C Lever

INDEX

BATTERY, BATTERIES
11, 18, 19, 20

LEVER 8, 9, 23

POWER, POWERED 11, 14, 18,19

SPRING 4, 5, 21, 22, 23

WHEEL, WHEELS
6, 12, 13, 14, 15, 23

Photocredits: Abbreviations: l-left, r-right, b-bottom, t-top, c-centre, m-middle.
All images are courtesy of Shutterstock.com.

Front Cover charles taylor. 1 – cristi180884. 2 - Ivonne Wierink. 3rt - Carsten Reisinger. 3mc - nevodka. 3rb - Delicate. 3lb - aastock. 4m - Deyan Georgiev. 4rb - wk1003mike. 5m - chonrawit boonprakob. 6lm - Zerbor. 6m - cristi180884. 7 - Tiplyashina Evgeniya. 8 - Robert Cumming. 9 - Sergey Lavrentev. 10l- Alex Dvihally. 10r - Gladskikh Tatiana 11 - nevodka. 11tr - auremar. 12 - Alexey Losevich. 13 - Tatyana Vyc. 13lm - Stephen Gibson. 14 - Stanislav_K. 15 - s_oleg. 16 - CroMary. 16lb - stefansonn. 17 - Luba V Nel. 17lb - Luba V Nel. 18 - Pressmaster. 19 - Pavel L Photo and Video. 20 - ISchmidt. 21 - Sergei Kolesnikov. 22tr - Daxiao Productions. 22bm - Brian A Jackson. 23tl - Lorelyn Medina. 23rm - StockPhotosArt. 23lb - AlexAvich